Meet my Neighbor

Meet my neighbor, the police officer

Marc Crabtree

Author and Photographer

Crabtree Publishing Company

www.crabtreebooks.com

Crabtree Publishing Company

Meet my neighbor, the police officer

Dedicated by Jenn Gellel:
To my beautiful niece Apollonia.

Author and photographer
Marc Crabtree

Editorial director
Kathy Middleton

Editor
Reagan Miller

Proofreader
Crystal Sikkens

Design and prepress technician
Samantha Crabtree

Production coordinator
Margaret Amy Salter

Print coordinator
Katherine Berti

Photographs
All photographs by Marc Crabtree except:
Shutterstock: pages 3, 24 (radio, handcuffs)

Library and Archives Canada Cataloguing in Publication

Crabtree, Marc
   Meet my neighbor, the police officer / Marc Crabtree.

(Meet my neighbor)
Issued also in electronic formats.
ISBN 978-0-7787-4561-7 (bound).--ISBN 978-0-7787-4566-2 (pbk.)

   1. Gellel, Jenn--Juvenile literature. 2. Police--Canada--
Biography--Juvenile literature. 3. Police--Juvenile literature.
I. Title. II. Series: Crabtree, Marc. Meet my neighbor.

HV7911.G45C73 2012   j363.2092   C2011-907915-1

Library of Congress Cataloging-in-Publication Data

Crabtree, Marc.
   Meet my neighbor, the police officer / Marc Crabtree.
       p. cm. -- (Meet my neighbor)
   Includes index.
   ISBN 978-0-7787-4561-7 (reinforced library binding : alk. paper) --
ISBN 978-0-7787-4566-2 (pbk. : alk. paper) -- ISBN 978-1-4271-7899-2
(electronic pdf) -- ISBN 978-1-4271-8014-8 (electronic html)
   1. Police--Juvenile literature. 2. Police patrol--Juvenile literature. I. Title.

HV7922.C73 2012
363.2--dc23
                                                          2011047833

Crabtree Publishing Company

Printed in Canada/012012/MA20111130

www.crabtreebooks.com   1-800-387-7650

Published in Canada
Crabtree Publishing
616 Welland Ave.
St. Catharines, Ontario
L2M 5V6

Published in the United States
Crabtree Publishing
PMB 59051
350 Fifth Avenue, 59th Floor
New York, New York 10118

Published in the United Kingdom
Crabtree Publishing
Maritime House
Basin Road North, Hove
BN41 1WR

Published in Australia
Crabtree Publishing
3 Charles Street
Coburg North
VIC 3058

Meet my Neighbor

Contents

Meet my neighbors, Jenn Gellel and her husband Brad. Jenn is a police officer.

Jenn works at a police station.

Police officers help to keep our communities safe. They make sure people follow the law.

6

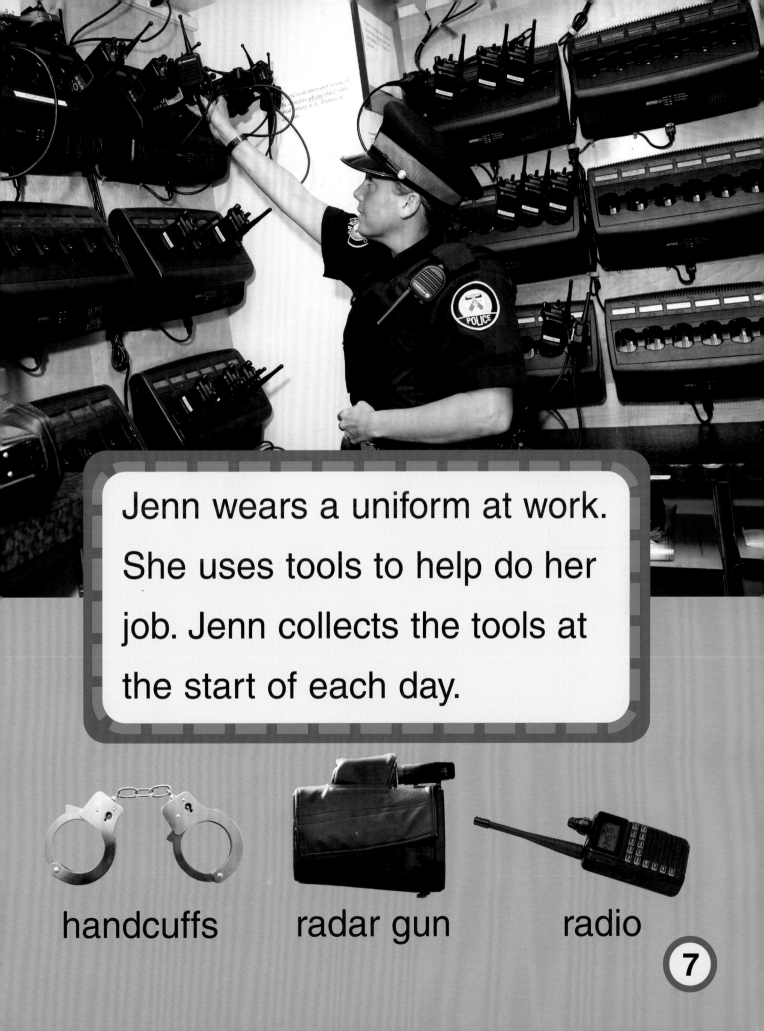

Jenn wears a uniform at work. She uses tools to help do her job. Jenn collects the tools at the start of each day.

handcuffs   radar gun   radio

Jenn meets with her inspector and the superintendent. They tell her what duties, or jobs, she will do today.

Jenn gets in her **police car**. There is a **radio** and a computer inside the car. She uses the radio to talk to other police officers and people at the police station.

Jenn uses the computer to look up information.

One of Jenn's jobs is to help make the roads safe. She makes sure people do not drive too fast.

Jenn uses a **radar gun**. The radar gun measures how fast cars are moving. It can show if a car is moving too fast.

Jenn gives this driver a **ticket** for driving too fast. She tells the driver to slow down and drive safely.

Jenn gets a call on her radio. The traffic lights are not working on a busy street. Jenn comes to direct traffic. She wears a brightly colored vest so drivers can see her easily.

Jenn gets another call on her radio. Someone is in trouble and needs help!